TO:

FROM:

A 12-STEP
STRATEGY FOR
SUCCESS

Create Your

yes

WHEN YOU
KEEP HEARING
NO

ANGELA MARIE HUTCHINSON

simple truths
▶ Small books. BIG IMPACT.

IGNITE READS
spark impact in just one hour

Photo Credits
Internal images © pages vi, 10, Westend61/Getty Images; page x, Work by Zach Dischner/Getty Images; page 17, Nodar Chernishev/EyeEm/Getty Images; page 32, Hinterhaus Productions/Getty Images; page 48, Vasyl Dolmatov/Getty Images; page 50, Mayur Kakade/Getty Images; page 60, Watchara Kharinta/Getty Images; page 72, Caiaimage/Paul Bradbury/Getty Images; page 74, champlifezy@gmail.com/Getty Images; pages 76, 80, 96, Hero Images/Getty Images; page 86, Caiaimage/Robert Daly/Getty Images; page 92, Caiaimage/Chris Ryan/Getty Images; page 102, 10'000 Hours/Getty Images; page 106, Jacobs Stock Photography/Getty Images; page 116, Hill Street Studios/Getty Images; page 120, Jessie Casson/Getty Images; page 136, JGI/Jamie Grill/Getty Images; page 140, Carlina Teteris/Getty Images; page 142, PeopleImages/Getty Images; page 144, Alistair Berg/Getty Images.
Internal images on page ix, 2, 4, 9, 14, 20, 24, 28, 36, 41, 42, 54, 64, 70, 78, 84, 108, 114, 122, 124, 130 have been provided by Pexels and Pixabay; these images are licensed under CC0 Creative Commons and have been released by the author for public use.

Published by Simple Truths, an imprint of Sourcebooks, Inc.
P.O. Box 4410, Naperville, Illinois 60567-4410
(630) 961-3900
sourcebooks.com

Printed and bound in China.
OGP 10 9 8 7 6 5 4 3 2 1

To coffee and green tea.
Without you, I'd still be writing this book.

Table of Contents

Introduction

WHEN YOU ARE FACED with rejection, do you cringe or thrive? The power of *no* is undeniable. While it's advantageous to embrace positive thinking and words of affirmation, understanding rejection is what allows you to redirect it.

In fact, it is often said that if you keep hearing no over and over again, your yes will eventually arrive. The idealistic concept of ninety-nine nos leading to a yes sounds hopeful. However, when I pursued having my screenplay, *Hollywood Chaos*, produced into a feature film, I sent hundreds of emails, attended dozens of networking events, and scheduled numerous meetings with power players—earning my ninety-nine nos in spades. Years and many more nos later, I still had no movie deal...until I produced it. Then, it aired on Hulu.

Sometimes your yes will never come—until you create it. In this book, I elaborate on the principles shared in my TEDx Talk, "Create Your Own Yes, When You Keep Hearing No." Creating your yes is a proven strategy to break through professional and personal barriers. Whether you are thriving or barely surviving, the twelve methods of creating opportunity that I reveal in this book will help you to achieve frequent wins and maintain your success.

Seize the journey!

1

Redirect the Rejection
| Navigating Nos

PURSUE A DREAM, GOAL, passion, or any opportunity, and you will undoubtedly hear no in one form or another. The visceral experience of rejection can hinder your ability to thrive both professionally and personally. I have coached dozens of professionals who became paralyzed from repeatedly hearing no. Regardless of their experience and skills, their careers remained stagnant. No matter how hard they worked, how many people they networked with, nothing

seemed to propel them to the next level. Perhaps you can relate to this rejection.

There are times when your life pursuits may seem hopeless, pointless, profitless, or otherwise daunting. Even in your darkest hour, you must firmly believe in your yes. In the city of Los Angeles, the mecca of glitz and glamour where dreams come true, the amount of rejection that it takes to achieve those dreams is never discussed. This observation is also consistent among other professions.

Lawyers take pride in the cases they've won.

Athletes celebrate their championships. Realtors toast when escrows close. Pharmaceutical reps are rewarded for their sales. No one brags about their losses. Sharing about our lack of success is not exactly a flattering social media post. #LOSING.

However, in Michael Jordan's "Failure" Nike commercial, he highlights his failures on the court, missing more than nine thousand basketball shots and losing nearly three hundred games. "I've failed over and over and over again in my life, and that is why I succeed," Jordan declares.

Massive Rejection

The more competitive the industry, the more massive the rejection. In covering the 90th Academy Awards as a commentator for BBC World News, I was reminded that only ninety producers have ever won the Best Picture Award, the most prestigious category of the Oscars ceremony. Yet an estimated five hundred thousand movies have been produced worldwide. That is a 0.018 percent success rate. Even if we round up, there is a 0 percent chance that a producer will receive an Oscar for Best Picture.

To catapult to success in your field, you must diligently navigate your nos. Throughout my entertainment career, I've had the opportunity to work as a talent agent and casting director. Getting signed by a talent agent is a hurdle even for talented actors. When casting an independent film, I rejected nearly twelve hundred actors for just one role. Dishing out rejection daily is a significant part of the casting process that I respect. By always having to say no, I gained a new perspective on the word.

When you hear a no, it's rarely personal. Don't take it that way. Rejection is a tool that teaches us, guides us, and sometimes redirects us to a path more aligned with our passion.

Redirect the No

How do you do that? Start by redirecting the rejection. You may need to become an entrepreneur or consider more of a business-savvy approach to traditional tasks. When I was submitting my screenplay, *Hollywood Chaos*, to power players all over town with the hope of it being produced, I was told no in one form or another. I sent emails, scheduled meetings, and networked with dozens of studio executives, literary managers, and film producers.

For almost ten years, I worked relentlessly toward getting my movie produced by a studio. I developed the script, secured interest from actors, joined arts organizations, and met with mentors and funding groups. I even rallied up a production team that was ready to produce the film upon obtaining interest from a studio or production company. Along the journey, I received a few maybes that eventually morphed into no.

The yes didn't come until I created it. By taking ownership of my career, I stopped yearning for validation from power players to produce my film. My creativity and business savvy were unleashed. I set a date for production, told everyone I knew my plan, created a crowdfunding campaign for donations, and pitched individual investors—even at my hair salon. Within a few months, I had raised enough money to produce the film for under $200,000 and obtained $65,000 in in-kind donations. I produced the movie and landed a distribution deal. *Hollywood Chaos* aired on Hulu and

is available on Amazon. The film was essentially funded by people who believed that I believed in my yes.

Now, not everyone needs to become an entrepreneur to create a yes. You may just need to transition your skills and experience into a different industry. A colleague of mine who works in human resources at Warner Bros. says it's important that job applicants fit into the culture of the department. If a company has a trendy and relaxed office environment and you wear a suit to the interview, you may not land the position.

Creating Opportunity

When interviewing for a job or seeking any opportunity, whether it's personal or professional, consider your value to the company. When someone gives you a yes, they want to know that working with you is mutually beneficial. So you must believe that and convey it to others. When you repeatedly hear no, it can either paralyze you or propel you. Creating your own yes is about owning the moment of opportunity.

At a job interview, good candidates bring a

polished résumé or work portfolio and are prepared for curveball questions. Exceptional candidates might also bring a SWOT analysis that they have performed to show the company's *strengths*, *weakness*, *opportunities*, and *threats*.

SWOT templates are easily accessible online. You can analyze the company based on its existing operational framework, or you can analyze yourself as it pertains to your ability to elevate a department. Even for an entry or midlevel position, presenting a SWOT analysis without being asked shows you are an asset to the company's brand.

Creating your own yes is about living your best life. To create means to bring into existence or to produce something that would not naturally evolve. I've created six books, two feature films, dozens of business ventures, a few companies, and even three young children. The power to create belongs to each of us.

Stop waiting for the phone to ring with your next opportunity. Stop obsessively checking your texts and emails, scouring your spam folder for life-altering good news. Stop spending hours liking your friends' social media highlights.

Balanced communication significantly increases the chances of advancing your career and accomplishing personal ambitions. There is no precise road map to success, but you can be 100 percent confident that rejection will undoubtedly find a path to you. Just don't let it block the intersection of your dreams taking flight.

2

Visualize Like a Pilot
| Periphery Success

PRACTICALLY EVERYONE KNOWS HOW to set and achieve goals. Individual goal setting ignites the drive to perform quality work. Equally as important are team achievements. Goal-focused teams are essential to maximizing productivity, whether launching a rocket, producing a business conference, or planning a family reunion cruise.

Even with a sincere commitment to clearly defined goals, failure is always a possibility. It's more common for people to fail than to succeed at achieving dream goals. Exceeding expectations is particularly rare. Why is this a phenomenon?

In the goal-creation phase, people resort to tunnel vision, which can lead to narrow-minded thinking and traditional objectives. Tunnel vision benefits tasks that require laser focus, such as threading a needle or shooting a basketball free throw.

The sharpest focus of our physical vision is directly in front of us. It's our field of vision that resembles a target. Outside our main line of vision is the peripheral vision, which is constantly active but not as a focal point. You can detect motion better with your peripheral vision, so homing in on it makes you more aware of what's happening around you.

Pilots are taught to use peripheral vision to steadily scan the sky for hazards such as light illusions or central blind spots. It takes practice, creativity, and concentration to recognize peripheral opportunities. You must make a conscious effort to use your mind and physical sight differently in visualizing goals and strategically planning areas of significance.

An important aspect of vision in general is that we can often look at something but not actually see it for what it is. There's an exercise I have performed with hundreds of people, and no one in any session has ever discovered the reveal until I explained it. Look at the picture below. Take a moment to discover a number that you see on the page.

Did you see the number 17? It's not in the picture that's in your tunnel vision. It's in your peripheral vision. Look again. The only real number that you can undisputedly identify on the previous page is at the bottom, in the middle—the actual page number.

It might feel like a trick, but the exercise showcases a common tendency among frustrated goal seekers. Their primary energy is devoted to what appears as a need based on instructions, rules, news, gossip, reports, or outdated experiences. However, what is needed to successfully complete the task is something entirely outside the box.

Understand the rules and how the game is played on your job or in a social situation. But know that the rules are a guide to help you thrive. If you are not thriving under those conditions, create change. Find a new avenue for how to gain camaraderie, increase sales, or expand productivity.

What appears as a need is not always what is necessary to complete a task. The tendency to look and not see is normal but can cause confusion. To avoid career collisions in your life, you must expand how you visualize, literally and metaphorically.

It's imperative to recognize that utilizing your peripheral vision does not mean you turn away from your main vision to check out the sidelines. That would entail refocusing your eyes to a different target point. When pilots land a plane at night, they primarily use their central vision while incorporating their peripheral vision with their eyes focused straight ahead.

Motion Detectors

Professional athletes have also mastered the balance of applying their tunnel and peripheral vision. Olympian runners never turn their head to size up opponents during a race. They do, however, use their peripheral sight to detect motion. When necessary, they exert more effort to propel their body forward. Strictly using tunnel vision or refocusing on peripheral throughout a long-distance race could be detrimental.

The same is true with your professional endeavors.

When you experience a massive fail, immediately tap into your peripheral vision. If you deprive yourself of vital information along your journey, you will miss out on peripheral opportunities.

Our peripheral vision is often used to detect faint light sources at night such as stars. Consider faint light sources as an opportunity with little or no pay. When you look at the sky, you might think you are looking at a star. If you download the SkyView app, it will show that you're looking at a planet. An opportunity may appear faint because of your vantage point.

Peripheral vision can be used to find a job or even a date. Pay attention to your environment. Consider the people you know distantly and those you know well, the places you frequently and rarely go, the content you enjoy and dislike, and especially home in on the physical roads of your day-to-day travel.

Here in Los Angeles, we have the luxury of accessing the 405 freeway, which is the most congested freeway in the United States. On any given day, there are over four hundred thousand cars traveling on the 405. One day while driving on the 405, there was a waving motion directing my attention to look, so I did. A dear college friend was driving in the adjacent car. He signaled me to get off at the next exit. We confirmed that our contact information for each other was current.

As I was driving away, I thought about the odds of seeing someone I knew on such a busy express-way. It wasn't as if we had attended the same event and then left at the same time. He had just moved to Los Angeles, and I had only been there a short couple of months.

Believe it or not, we started hanging out frequently after that day. Now, Arthur and I have been married for fifteen years. Creating your own yes means producing unforgettable experiences and recognizing the best people to help you thrive and expand your vision.

3

Focus on Inchstones
| Achieving Milestones

REJECTIONS ARE THE TRAINING wheels for success. Receiving a no is an opportunity to propel your life forward. But you must fundamentally absorb the merit of forward movement.

In considering social movements, there isn't always a massive goal or milestone. End results evolve based on economic, political, and social circumstances. The ultimate victory of a movement is determined by sustainable actions. Even the most successful campaigns experience setbacks or countermovements, yet new innovative leaders arise, and social movements continue to significantly impact our world with proven solutions. When a movement stands the test of time, it is deemed a success.

The framework for success in any industry depends on who you ask. In ball sports, movement and possession are dominant forces. According to Orison Swett Marden, a renowned author who founded *SUCCESS* magazine, success is not measured by accomplishments but by the opposition encountered.

Measuring Success

It's difficult to avoid measuring success in our society, from the Oscars to the Grammys to the countless corporate and trailblazer awards given throughout the year. The measurement of success should be a personal expression of the vision for your career, health, finances, relationships, and overall life experiences.

I once asked my seven-year-old daughter how to measure success. She suggested a ruler. Yes, how adorable. But let's take a moment to examine success using an inch-by-inch principle.

How many inches are there in a mile? 63,360. Imagine if it took 63,360 actions to reach every career milestone. When track stars or marathon runners prepare for a race, they undergo extreme task-oriented preparation. Knowing that you have to accomplish steps to achieve a goal is certainly not a new concept. However, zeroing in on "inchstones" can elevate your milestones and reduce the rejection that you're facing in life.

Milestones vs. Inchstones

Inchstones are small tasks within your control. Losing five pounds is a small goal, but it is not necessarily in your control. Don't think of it as an inchstone. You can control whether you do five burpee jump-ups today. That's an inchstone. Inchstones are daily wins. Milestones are the big wins: to be the top salesperson, get married or pregnant, retire early, become a millionaire by a certain age, buy a business, or reach a performance benchmark.

Milestones are goals that you hope to achieve, but you may not due to various hindrances. Inchstones are the daily or weekly goals that you can undoubtedly and promptly accomplish without rejection. Examples of inchstones are sending emails to schedule informational meetings, making a certain number of phone calls, uploading finished content to YouTube or a blog, sending ten connection requests on LinkedIn, joining two new Facebook groups in a different state, or subscribing to a local trade publication.

Most people use tunnel vision to determine their milestones, so they are easier to come up with than inchstones. When you think about the actual steps you may need to take to achieve a milestone, it can be mind-boggling and overwhelming. It will require utilizing your peripheral vision. Task mapping on a poster board may minimize the abundance of possibilities.

If it did take 63,360 actions to achieve life milestones, you would go crazy trying to strategize for every niche goal. While it is helpful to launch with a plan, it's detrimental to get stuck in the planning phase. So trust your instincts throughout the process of pinpointing controllable actions you can take right now.

To achieve success, you must either reach your goals or have movement toward them. The word *success* is searched on Google far more times than the word *progress*. Most people focus on achieving success instead of achieving progress.

Progress is forward movement toward a destination. To accomplish a milestone in business or any facet of life, progress should be the primary target. The key to achieving a milestone is forward movement toward your goal, but you don't necessarily have to accomplish the intended goal. The golden key to success is continual progress.

Success varies due to numerous factors. Making an extra five thousand dollars this month, purchasing a used car with cash, increasing sales by 5 percent, taking on a second job when you have a strenuous

"I've missed more than nine thousand shots in my career. I've lost almost three hundred games. Twenty-six times, I've been trusted to take the game-winning shot and missed. I've failed over and over and over again in my life. And that is why I succeed."

—MICHAEL JORDAN

full-time position, or traveling the world but still living with a roommate may be considered a success to some but not to everyone. Progress, however, is undeniable. If you are moving forward toward your goal, that defines progress.

If you are living with a roommate but recently paid off your credit card debt and purchased a car with cash, well, you're not doing too shabby if your milestone is to be debt-free by the end of the year, which might encourage your roommate to follow your path of financial freedom.

The standard barometer for success is impact. Even *Forbes* magazine doesn't publish a list of "the most successful." Success is a metric used to highlight high-net-worth individuals who have influence and power. When classifying your influence and power, consider your inchstones. Evaluate how they will impact you or your target population.

The path to funding success is seed money and small pilot projects or short-term ventures. If a filmmaker's goal is to raise $1 million for an independent feature film, they should first attempt to raise $1,000 to produce a short film or web series. Whether a campaign is fully or partially funded does not determine the success for raising future capital. The process of analyzing a funding campaign is valuable in determining new benchmarks based on past performance.

Productive inchstones for raising capital or charity donations are frequent participation in webinars outside your field and in different states. Learn the diverse strategies and technology tools that charities, technology start-ups, or investment firms are utilizing to secure funding.

Milestones are exciting to think about and talk about, but they are often difficult to achieve because you may lack the knowledge, contacts, or financial resources. Inchstones are practically the opposite— you have nearly everything you need to complete these goals. Continually accomplishing inchstones leads to periphery success.

4

Categorize the No
| Breaking Barriers

NEVER IGNORE NO. IT'S detrimental to disregard rejection. Everyone is exposed to it. No one is immune from it. Rejection is defined in three functions: the act of rejecting, the state of being rejected, and medical rejections related to our immune systems.

A UCLA survey reported that a toddler hears no over four hundred times a day. By the time we are adults, you would think that no would not affect our confidence. What appears to happen is that as children, we are resilient and remain persistent, asking again and again to get the yes. Then as adults, we start to become more accepting of no. We must respect the word in many cases so as not to cross appropriate boundaries. Aside from those situations, determine the type of no you are hearing. Using that insight, brainstorm how to formulate a yes.

There are many versions of what a no can look like depending on the subject matter. Appreciating rejection can stimulate ideas on how to break a barrier.

Types of Rejection

Let's lightly explore rejection as it pertains to our immune systems. There are three distinct types of rejection involved with transplanted organs: hyperacute rejection, acute rejection, and chronic rejection.

An example of hyperacute rejection is a recipient given the wrong blood type. If you have a salsa recipe and aim for distribution at a burger chain, rejection will occur immediately unless you pitch a Mexican-style burger.

With acute rejection, all recipients of a transplant experience a level of rejection. Consider this the daily no. Polite conversational rejections are the easiest to face as both the recipient or deliverer. A barista suggests a new breakfast menu item to complement your cold brew coffee, but you decline by ordering your usual cranberry scone. "No, but thank you" rejections for the most part require no form of redirection. At a sales pitch meeting, the prospective client offers you a bottled water, but you politely decline because you have one in your purse. A simple no is swiftly dished out and easily digested.

Chronic rejection is the last type and takes place over many years. This occurs when the body's immune system slowly damages the transplanted organ. In the personal space, chronic rejection is when you have tried for over ten years like I did to pursue a dream. When you keep getting closer yet failing, it gradually damages your confidence and aspiration—if you allow it.

In chronic rejection, there is no available treatment; a patient must receive a new organ. A similar principle applies to life's rejections. When you experience massive failure in your finances, family life, job, or health, you must renew your mind, even if it's late in your life. Recognize that failing forward is powerful and contagious.

Why the Nos?

When determining how to respond to a no, consider the reasons people say no:

- ▶ Bad timing
- ▶ Lack of clarity
- ▶ Requires in-depth review
- ▶ Bound by rules or protocol
- ▶ Approval needed but unavailable
- ▶ Too busy to thoroughly consider

A corporation may not want or even need your business product or service, but it's not about their no. It's about your yes. Consider what prompts you to say yes. Time deficiency is a common motive for rejection. The average professional receives two hundred emails per day. In seeking a response from a prominent executive, you can effortlessly be ignored or receive a quick decline out of convenience. The point is, sometimes rejection isn't personal. But it can be, due to a lack of refinement. Evaluate your inquiry for a yes to ensure it's well-deserved and refined. If you discover that more exploration is needed to perfect your ask, that's okay. Proposing a seed of an idea, trial program, pilot project, or soft product launch can be advantageous in gaining the momentum for a prospective opportunity.

Rejection vs. Silence

Silence can feel like a passive-aggressive form of rejection. In the entertainment industry, some film producers are content if they haven't heard back from an investor because there is hope that the project is still in consideration. Being on the radar provides a sense of satisfaction. However, an upfront, quick no presents an opportunity to implement strategies for creating the yes. When an idea has been thoroughly considered for weeks and months by various teams, it can be difficult to obtain reconsiderations without drastic changes to what was initially presented.

Silence is not always better. Rejection is an effective communication technique. Repeatedly hearing no might stink at first. According to neuroscience, if you keep experiencing an unpleasant smell, your sense of smell adapts, and it no longer has an effect. Your sense of smell becomes desensitized to prevent your body's nervous system from overloading. When you constantly experience rejection, allow your mind to adapt to the point where it influences you to create an opportunity for yourself and others.

Rejection in Relationships

Even with intimate relationships, business principles can apply. As a social media professor, my students are amused when I suggest utilizing a SWOT analysis in dating. The purpose of such an analysis is to determine everything that could impact the success of a fruitful partnership. While doing a SWOT sounds hilarious, marriage as a lifetime journey takes a great deal of effort to survive, just as any start-up venture takes passion, sacrifices, and commitment.

When deciding on a long-term relationship or business partnership, identify the strengths and weaknesses of the candidate, along with opportunities that may be presented to elevate you professionally or personally, and lastly any threats that may prevent the relationship from thriving. Paying close attention to how people deal with rejection in business and in life may reveal how they deal with close relationships. Failure to realistically consider these internal and external factors

can lead to a failed relationship. Luckily, even if you are already in a committed relationship or business collaboration and you did not perform a SWOT analysis, it's not too late and may even better serve your needs, because you have in-depth experiences to draw from as you strengthen the existing relationship.

5

Identify Advocates
| Collaborative Pursuits

ADVANCEMENT AND PERSONAL GROWTH are intricate parts of every career trajectory. Thriving professionals who have not experienced a mentor relationship may question the value of mentoring as well as have difficulty in identifying a suitable mentor or career coach. Even *Fortune* 500 companies and small businesses struggle to find innovative strategists.

Through my years of coaching professionals and serving as a business consultant, far too often, the term *mentorship* is not thoroughly understood. Therefore, mentors are underutilized, as are partnerships. It's not always about who you know but who knows you.

The best types of mentors are those who become sponsors, individuals who financially contribute to your success. A sponsor may invest, help you obtain a grant or loan, or donate to your crowdfunding campaign without expectations of a financial return. A sponsor may be an influencer in a niche space or an expert with millions of Instagram followers or YouTube subscribers. They can retweet a post about your product or service or share the crowdfunding campaign to their following or email list.

Mentors in your field can be useful, but think outside the box. Publicists, bloggers, and journalists make great mentors because they stay abreast of news, conferences, and industry trends. With the quantity of books and digital content available, deciding which content to consume can be a headache. Mentors who you trust can alleviate that stress by sharing their go-to magazines or news sources. A favorite publication of mine is *CSQ*, published by a powerful and integrated media company. It's a quarterly magazine that profiles prominent leaders and offers substantive advisory articles written by C-Suite business executives. Also consider publications that may be out of print and search for digital archives.

Finding a Mentor

- Mentors do not have to live in the same state.
- Mentors can be peers, younger than you, or your boss.
- Mentors do not have to know you.
- Mentors can work at your company or not.
- Mentors do not have to be your employer.
- Mentors do not have to be in the same field.
- You can have multiple mentors.
- Mentors can communicate solely via email, phone, or social media.

When you read the latest issue of *Fast Company* and wonder why your business hasn't achieved mind-blowing success or surpassed customer expectations, implement the guidance of a mentor or collaborative business expert.

Perhaps you've been grinding at your goals and hoping to attract a mentor. You may have asked numerous times, but your requests are ignored or declined. Research SCORE, the nation's largest network of business experts who volunteer their time to help professionals like you gain career momentum. As a partner of the U.S. Small Business Administration, SCORE has helped more than ten million entrepreneurs through mentoring and free business resources.

Facebook COO Sheryl Sandberg attributes much of her success to a college professor who served as a mentor and a sponsor who played a pivotal role in her career. It was the advice of another mentor that encouraged Sheryl to work for Mark Zuckerberg, even though she would be reporting to a younger boss.

When I was interviewed by *Rolling Out* magazine, I was asked to name an ideal mentor if it could be anyone in the world. While of course Oprah would be awesome, as a social media professor, I find that the college students I teach are incredibly resourceful. Clueing in on your peripheral resources can be pivotal to achieving progress. The little girl I used to babysit is currently a human resource executive at Facebook.

Don't discount younger mentors if they have mastered a craft or skill or have access to unique resources that align with your vision.

If you still aren't comfortable with one-on-one mentor relationships, consider applying to the hundreds of fellowships available through companies and membership-based organizations or angel investor funding programs such as start-up accelerators or incubators. Google and LinkedIn are the best resources to scout which programs are best suited for your career path.

It's also incredibly useful to connect with professionals who have achieved goals similar to those on your vision board. Home in on the small print within their bios and look for a connection to charities they support, the college they attended, or similar organization affiliations.

Investing the Time

When researching mentors, invest the time to fully investigate their background, including any books or articles they have authored. In trying to secure an investor to buy a struggling performing arts theater, a budding entrepreneur was referred to an investor by a peer mentor. In the first email to the investor, the entrepreneur boldly asked for seed funds of $50,000.

Due to the close relationship that the investor had with the referral, the investor immediately responded to the entrepreneur, saying, "Hi, Marie. I would be happy to give you all the seed funds *if* you can confidently say that you read the book I wrote on owning a theater."

When you haven't read the book, let alone even know he wrote one, how do you reply to that email?

Because the entrepreneur was very green, she froze by saying, "I have not read your book, but I just purchased and will promptly read it. Thank you for your time."

A frequently rejected entrepreneur used to creating their own yes would have waited two days to respond while either ordering the book on Amazon overnight or going into every single bookstore to find the hard copy. Then they would have read every word of the book and responded with, "Yes, I have read your book. Attached is a report on my key takeaways. Thank you so much. I look forward to discussing my initial inquiry."

The seasoned entrepreneur who values time

would have performed due diligence. They would have read the book before contacting the investor. Get to know your advocates online before they get to know you. It's only fair, wouldn't you say, for $50,000?

Once you have selected strong advocates, nurture those relationships by specifying your dilemmas. Keep in mind that asking someone to mentor or sponsor you usually isn't the best strategy, because it places too much pressure on a prominent person. Some mentorships develop organically over extended periods of time. In those scenarios, speak up about your needs.

A mentor doesn't expect you to know why you aren't achieving your goals. Trial and error play a significant role in business, science, and our economy. It's unreasonable to expect advocates to invest their time, knowledge, or resources when you have not yet rigorously tested your ability or systematically tried to solve your problems. Identifying advocates for your personal brand or business can generate financial success and ignite your productivity.

6

Erase What You Know Beyond the Status Quo

"YOU MUST CRAWL BEFORE you walk" is a familiar saying that expresses the concept of learning the basics before going to the next level. If you Google that phrase along with the word *success*, you'll find dozens of articles to validate this concept. Whether it's proving your contribution to a team project to receive a promotion or laying a strong foundation to sustain a business, there's a consensus that you must succeed in the first step in order to reach the second step. Let's challenge this theory by thinking beyond the status quo.

When my firstborn son was around ten months old, he had not yet crawled. Initially, our family was concerned that he might be a slow learner. But one day, he spontaneously pulled himself up and started walking. To reiterate, prior to our son's first steps, he had never once crawled. While I'd like to think he was a baby genius, he is not alone. According to an Australian study, about 10 percent of toddlers do not crawl before they walk. However, a few other studies suggest that if a child does not learn to crawl first, they may have difficulty concentrating, struggle with mathematical concepts, and possibly develop ADD/ADHD.

My son is quite the opposite, with concentration being one of his greatest assets. He has scored over 100 percent on tests and was placed in the accelerated math group in his fourth-grade class. Even with my industrial and operations engineering bachelor's degree from the University of Michigan, my son has actually guided me through grasping the new common core math concepts that are different from how I learned mathematics in the '90s.

From the time we are children, we are trained to color between the lines. As teenagers, we are taught to drive between the lines. As college students, we are told to master a skill, because a jack-of-all-trades is a master of none.

While I do have a tremendous amount of respect for experts who have mastered their craft, the requirement for success is not mastery. It's resiliency. It's originality. To create your own yes, you must continuously pursue innovative solutions.

Unconventional Logic

On a rainy day in Chicago when I was young, my mother and I dashed into Pizza Hut to get our meat lover's pizza. Our clothes were drenched when we returned to the car. I wondered why the pizzeria didn't have a drive-thru. When I asked my mother, she told me that pizzas take too long to make and wouldn't be ready quickly enough for a drive-thru. I accepted that logic. Perhaps had I challenged that thought, I could have invented Pizza Hut's existing drive-thru, which serves personal pan pizzas and bread sticks.

Temporarily erase what you know. This may involve dissecting or disregarding daily inspirational quotes, motivational speeches, and even wise advice from family, mentors, and colleagues. To start with a clean slate of thinking about how to tackle a rejected goal or unfinished task, you'll need to first rely on your instincts.

If you're a visual person like myself, buy a poster board and write down the goal, even if it's been rejected numerous times. Then you'll need to brainstorm clever ways to achieve your pursuits. Going beyond the status quo entails transformational thinking but not necessarily grandiose ideas. Even a simple gesture can accelerate your career trajectory.

Extraordinary Steps

I recall when the surprising success of Tyler Perry's first theatrically released film, *Diary of a Mad Black Woman*, was covered in the *Hollywood Reporter*, an entertainment trade publication. The president of Lionsgate mentioned that the studio was actively seeking similar scripts from diverse writers. At the time, I had a screenplay, *Hollywood Chaos*, that I had written and was pitching around town. The story had a similar tone to Perry's film, so I decided to contact the Lionsgate president.

Now, entertainment executives are instructed by their companies not to respond to unsolicited submissions for legal reasons. An unsolicited email typically gets forwarded to the legal department. I know this to be true because I have received a plethora of rejection letters, stating that my material was unsolicited, since it was not requested, and was therefore never reviewed.

To be taken seriously, the project should be represented by an agent, manager, or prominent attorney. Film school professors instruct students to follow the traditional routes of submitting their work by securing a literary agent. This infrastructure protects writers from their ideas being stolen and protects studios when they have similar projects already in development.

I did not personally know the president of Lionsgate, and I did not have literary representation that could contact him on my behalf. I scoured the Internet for his email address. Instead, I found the email to a publicity executive who worked at Lionsgate. Then I used the same format to guess the president's email address—first initial and last name @lionsgate.com. I sent a brief email mentioning his quote in the article and suggested that he read my script.

To my surprise, he responded in minutes and had cc'd several of his executives. They followed up with me that same day. I completed the required submission release form and emailed over my script. They read it and passed, but they invited me for a meeting at the studio to learn more about my goals as a filmmaker. All because I activated the *Hollywood Reporter*.

The Catch-22

Give yourself permission to frequently try the impossible. Throughout your success journey, colleagues, family members, and even mentors you genuinely trust may suggest that you need to have something that you don't have to get what you want.

This is the catch-22 syndrome: to launch a business, you need capital. To get the capital, you need to generate revenue. To generate revenue, you need a loan. To get the loan, you need assets or a track record, which may be difficult to provide for a new venture.

Don't allow this double-edged sword to hinder you from moving forward. If you need funding, be sure to purchase a subscription to *Fast Company*, *Inc.*, *Money*, or *Kiplinger's Personal Finance* as well as local publications that are specific to your city or community, such as a business journal or chamber of commerce magazine.

The general public reads magazine articles to gain new insights. To go beyond the status quo, I challenge you to activate the content that you read. Allow the relevant information from articles and social media posts to permeate your life. I have an IT guru friend in San Francisco who received a post on social media about a power brunch with the most elite influencers in the city. The ticket was priced into the thousands. He tweeted the organizers a positive comment and offered to volunteer at the event. They agreed. He attended the event for free and was assigned as a greeter, which hardly involved work for his congenial personality. Where there is a will, there is a way indeed—but you may need to create it.

7

Generate Sustainability
| Brand vs. Identity

OVER 5 BILLION VIDEOS are watched on YouTube every day. Nearly 480 million products are available on Amazon. According to the U.S. Small Business Association, six hundred thousand companies launch every year. These stats almost make the three hundred available car models to choose from an opportunity for growth, until compared with the sixty models in the 1950s, when 58 million cars were sold.

Distinguishing your brand in a robust marketplace

is imperative to remain competitive. For a Super Bowl ad campaign, Kia employed socks to promote a new car model. The collaboration was between Kia, the sock marketer Stance, and Influential, an influencer platform. Kia hired actor Christopher Walken as the celebrity talent for the campaign. For the television commercial, Walken convinces a beige-sock-wearing businessman that he needs pizzazz. He gives the guy a pair of radical socks, comparing them to Kia's newest midsize sedan as a "natural fit."

Throughout the campaign, Kia sent the socks to one hundred social media influencers who then posted about the socks to their friends and followers. If socks are a vehicle to market a vehicle, what will you cultivate to stand out?

Bold 360°

In the advertising industry, a 360-degree campaign is implemented to engage and interact with customers from various access points. Campaign elements will include social media posts to spark viral buzz, trade shows for live interactions with consumers, and bold collaborations to garner media attention.

Observing how advertising agencies market their clients' products and services provides innovative solutions to redirecting your rejection. An integrated 360-degree marketing and branding strategy can help you discover the uniqueness of your brand and identity.

Brand vs. Identity

Establishing a clearly defined brand and identity is an asset in strategic planning. Your identity is who you are without question. Your brand is how you are perceived. Your business name reflects your identity. Your website with offered products should noticeably echo your brand.

Every successful company has a recognizable color scheme, logo, and consistent visual design elements. What if a company changed their color scheme every day on their website? What if their employees also had different color business cards? What if a prominent branded company purchased 365 domains, and every day, their domain address was different? That's going beyond a different splash home page. To gain and retain traction in an evolving marketplace of saturated content, products, and services, find a way to make your brand indispensable.

You don't have to be a marketing expert to launch ground-breaking campaigns, although consulting with a firm might help stir up cool concepts. Regardless, a vantage point of how your customer can authentically connect with your brand is required. Spotting distin-guishable advertising campaigns is an effortless way to keep a pulse on consumer buzz and new business-to-business models. On a personal level, your brand can attract strong advocates and supporters. Your wardrobe style and branding by association are also powerful tools.

Social Media Auditing

Performing a social media audit is another optimal tool to understand who you are, how people view you, and what added value you are contributing to society—whether it's humor, business strategy, the facts of life, healthy habits, daily inspiration, or even constant complaints. You can audit your social media sites as an individual, company, or target audiences.

Social media audits can be simple with just a two-page overview or as extensive as a lengthy

PowerPoint. Hiring a consultant to perform an audit is a pragmatic way to develop efficient campaigns, similar to how advertising agencies produce engaging Super Bowl commercials.

In a cluttered marketplace, more of the same may not get you fired, but it definitely won't get you hired. Preserve the past, but avoid lingering there with these thoughts:

- "In college, we used to…"
- "When we first got married, you…"
- "Last year, our profits were…"
- "Yesterday, we…"

Innovation is today's opportunity to create a thriving tomorrow. If you want uber success, creating the next Uber isn't going to win you a Visionary of the Year award. To generate sustainability in the marketplace as a business, connect consumers to your brand and identity via immersive experiences. As a professional, regularly contribute to the convergence of art, business, science, and technology. Continue to elevate others amid their rejections. If you take ordinary steps within untraditional environments, you'll obtain extraordinary results.

8

Get Off the Hamster Wheel | Mediocre Living

ARE YOU MOVING AT lightning speed toward your vision but not getting ahead at work or in life? You're likely on a hamster wheel. Hop off before you burn out or exhaust yourself of mediocre living. You can do everything right and still face rejection.

You can be the best candidate, spouse, parent, business partner, or employee. Less skilled and talented people frequently get ahead in life. Success doesn't discriminate. It's not always about hard work, determination, and hustle.

Getting out of the limbo phase requires strategy. But first, throw a party! Before you abruptly quit your dead-end job, sell your declining business, or divorce your second husband, pat yourself on the back for what you have accomplished in your struggle areas.

Don't be shy about the celebration either. If you or your business is in any way better off today than last year or a decade ago, congratulate yourself for the trails you have blazed. There is a time to work, to play, and to celebrate. When you recognize the achievements of yourself and others, you'll gain clarity about your objectives. Celebrating can also provide your team with renewed energy to better support your mission through the long haul.

Tenacity vs. Resiliency

When you think about tenacity, what comes to mind is a person who pushes forward at all costs no matter how tough the journey. A tenacious professional endures extreme workplace turmoil, such as a verbally abusive manager, prolonged salary increases, or disgruntled team environments. Tenacity is a desirable trait, but only when coupled with the ability to transcend challenges.

Stamina alone can be crippling, because you may

endure unnecessary pain and suffering. Embracing mental toughness does not always lead to progress. Resilience is what breaks barriers. Rejection itself can never be eliminated. However, a rapid, well-thought-out response to no sets the groundwork to maintain happiness while in pursuit of milestones.

Now, you may be working smart, executing a plan with immense effort and productivity. Yet your professional or personal trajectory is stagnant. When this occurs, find an alternative route to keep your goals in motion, even if it's slow motion.

First, pinpoint a target, then determine whether stamina or speed is required to reach the goal. This process leads to finding the middle ground of where rejection and success intersect. My son who never crawled as a toddler is intrigued by the cheetah and gazelle relationship. It's also a creditable analogy for assessing the dominant trait needed to accomplish goals.

Stamina and Speed

It's a familiar fact that cheetahs are the fastest land animal and that gazelles have great stamina, which allows them to sometimes outrun a preying cheetah. Stamina is a fundamental attribute to surviving in life, but so is speed. You may be hearing no because you are focusing on your stamina when you need to concentrate on speed, or vice versa.

In the animal kingdom, animals are either sprinters or marathon runners. The cheetah is capable of short

bursts of explosive speed, while the gazelle sustains its speed, allowing it to sometimes outrun the cheetah. It's all about timing.

A cheetah's speed has limited range. If it runs for too fast for too long, it will die. A gazelle has a cooler brain temperature, which allows it to maintain a higher speed without overheating. Whether or not the gazelle outruns the cheetah depends significantly on the cheetah's starting point. Now, we've heard the saying it doesn't matter where you start but where you finish. That's partially true, but sometimes, the start is a matter of life or death. That's why it's so important to challenge what we think we know and consider our cookie-cutter circumstances.

It's advantageous to conceptualize if you operate like a cheetah or a gazelle. But it's vital to know which trait is most beneficial to accomplishing your target goal. Is the task that you are pursuing a cheetah goal or a gazelle goal?

If you're a single mother and need to secure a babysitter for a week, cheetah goals are harder without a support system or financial resources. It doesn't mean you can't win. Your temporary deficiency prepares and qualifies you to obtain dynamic opportunities.

Writing a five-hundred-word article to post on LinkedIn, that's a cheetah goal. In comparison, creating an investor pitch deck and business plan from scratch, that's a gazelle goal. Consider your industry's climate, time factors, and financial resources easily accessible to you.

Stamina and speed are both valuable, but which one carries a higher weight depends on the goal or project. You may be built to endure like a gazelle, but speed is necessary to run a short distance race. The fastest distance runner and sprinter are often not the same Olympian.

Just as a gazelle relies on its brain to escape predators, you must rely on yours to escape being the prey of rejection. If you are lacking monetary resources, explore additional revenue streams or recreate goals that align with a gazelle lifestyle for this season of your life. Don't let slow motion drive you to quit. It's okay to reroute your life and reinvent your goals.

Stamina and speed are just a few of the attributes that come into play in competitive environments. Maybe it's analyzing bulldog determination or Bengal tiger strength. Assessing strengths and weaknesses is key to positioning yourself for curveball opportunities.

Even once you have a clear picture of your ideal targets and the skills needed for the execution, some aspects of your plan may linger as to be determined, or TBD. And that's okay. Broadly used in event planning, TBD indicates that although something is scheduled or expected to happen, an aspect remains to be determined, arranged, or confirmed.

Since variables are inevitable in life, embrace the obstacles that you face. Let adversity drive you to excel. Never allow the burnouts to weaken your zeal. Get aligned with your purpose by networking and joining organizations for professional and personal development. Doing so will help the TBDs in your life become placeholders for victories.

q

Bulletproof Your Mind
| Got ICE?

LIFE-THREATENING ILLNESSES, DEATH OF loved ones, divorces, tragedies, caregiving for aging parents, and other work-life balance issues from the past or present can hinder your ability to maximize success. Moderate daily stressors can also debilitate your progress, such as bad work days, parental fatigue, social anxiety, body aches, family disputes, and financial pressures.

No matter how distressing your situation, bullet-proof your mind. How? First, structure how you allocate your attention, then shift your mindset from scarcity to abundance. Give purpose and meaning to not only your life goals but also your daily responsibilities.

You may have recently lost a loved one and feel like quitting your weight loss plan or become distracted from starting a business venture. Sticking to your body goals and blogging about the process may encourage your followers to strive toward a fit lifestyle. Attaining a business benchmark may be the difference in someone else's family being able to afford a heart transplant based on a job with health benefits that your company will provide when hitting a certain profit margin.

Adversity Blues

Hitting rock bottom or a version of it can radically transform your personal life and catapult your business. I know all about fatigue as a mother of three young children. When I once glanced at a college friend's Facebook post of earning a master's degree when she has ten kids, my fatigue transitioned into a pointless complaint. Hopefully, yours does too.

Someone in the world would like to have the life that you have carved out. That's not to say you should happily endure hardships. Let's get real. Life is tough. Sometimes the infrequent bad times overshadow the frequent good times.

You may be in a toxic relationship or lack stable companionship. Perhaps you are dissatisfied with how your life has turned out thus far. You may be saddened that you don't know your life's purpose or are overwhelmed by all that you could do. With your range of talents or interests, you still can't seem to start and finish anything worthy, even though you know exactly what you want out of life.

Your rocky childhood or family secrets may spiral your mind into feeling unworthy. Overwhelmingly hearing no or silent rejections may have triggered you to be frustrated. Maybe you tried to move on from your dream. But it refuses to die, no matter how diligently you try to shake it off. Listen up. The life that you desire is in front of you. Create it.

If that sounds overwhelming, hire a business consultant to help execute your vision. If it's more of a personal goal, find a life coach, career coach, or dear friend to help you brainstorm practical ways to achieve progress amid your drama.

A real-life crisis may contribute to your hindrances, but a pessimistic belief system may be the real culprit. Often, pessimism is the dominant barrier. It can temporarily stunt success of the most dynamic leader. We all have the gift of life, which means we are tasked with living it abundantly. #InItToWinIt

At the age of eight, I was kidnapped by a stranger for less than a minute. In those life-altering seconds, I had to make a split-second decision that ultimately changed the course of my life forever. I decided to leap out of a moving vehicle, bruising my body (but minor cuts compared to whatever my kidnapper had in mind). After the rusty blue car sped away from my school, within a few minutes, I was surrounded by my principal, police officers, and EMTs. Soon after, I returned home to my parents. From that day on, I better understood the meaning of tomorrow not being promised.

Foundation Building

Whether it's a negative or challenging situation demanding your attention, it's never too late to bullet-proof your mind with ICE. Typically, ice is defined as frozen water and appears in various forms such as an iceberg, glacier, or ice cube. The chemical formula for ice is H_2O, which is the bond formation of two hydrogen atoms and one oxygen atom. This bond is critical in controlling the structure of ice.

Similarly, a crucial component to taking control of

your career, your business, or your life is to form a bond with solid elements. In other words, build your goals on ICE (integrity, creativity, and enthusiasm).

The next time your dream is tested by rejection letters, insufficient funds, failed relationships, or ignored phone calls and emails, resort to your ICE. If your integrity, creativity, and enthusiasm are intact, continue striving. However, if you feel depressed, do *not* hang in there! That's dangerous territory. It's better to fall and get back up again than to hang on to hopelessness or to invest your time in a situation that's not well-suited for you.

Count on your ICE. It will never mislead you. An unusual property of ice is that the solid is less dense than water, which allows it to float instead of sink. As the architect to your life, you must build your dreams on the foundation of ICE. Doing so will ensure that your integrity, creativity, and enthusiasm will not drown in the murky waters of fear, anxiety, and worry.

Now, you may question the validity of building

upon a substance that is known to melt. You must structure your thinking like the Persian engineers who mastered the technique of keeping ice from melting in the desert. The environment they created through massive refrigerated structures underground kept the ice cold even in the hottest temperatures. As it relates to life, surround yourself in socially supportive environments alongside positive professionals who are aligned with similar goals, such as members of networking organizations and guilds.

Accidents and storms are inevitable. In times of uncertainty and testing phases, pushing through adversity builds the foundation for unapologetic success. When bulletproofing your mind, you open space to see open doors.

If your dream has already slipped away, rebuild it. If you're on the verge of quitting, get some *hielo*, *glace*, *gelo*, *eis*, *is*—and say yes to "Got ICE?"

10

Open the Door
The Art of Waiting

IN SEEKING OPPORTUNITY, MOMENTS of self-doubt and frustration may arise. Just don't get comfortable waiting for someone to open an automatic sliding door. Be proactive in your search. Yes, patience is a virtue. Occasionally, people and opportunities will find you. If you are tired of hearing crickets, then do something about it. There is an art to waiting; it's called productive patience. Waiting when you don't have to is an example of self-imposed rejection.

Why Lines Form

How do you know if you are unnecessarily waiting? Exploring the formation of lines may offer a fresh outlook. Lines form for two reasons: a sincere need for the line, or the assumption that you are required to wait for what you want. The best example deals with the women's restroom. For whatever reason, maybe not enough female architects, there are never enough stalls.

Inside a picturesque five-thousand-seat venue in

Los Angeles, there is a ground-floor bathroom with ten individual stalls. When I entered the bathroom, there was a line of at least seven women. After patiently waiting, I noticed, like others had, that the line was not moving. The women murmured about how people were taking forever. A couple of women hinted at wanting to glance under the stalls to see if there were feet. No one did—except me. I walked to the front of the line and scanned underneath. Guess what? Every single one of those ten stalls was empty.

Believe it or not, educated and beautiful women were waiting in line for absolutely no reason. I immediately started directing the women who were ahead of me to the stalls. Some of them, even though they had seen me look under, were hesitant to push the door open. Eventually, it was my turn. As I exited the restroom, the line had reformed, but it was moving like it should have been in the first place.

I'm not sure if that moment was as significant to each woman. It was a bathroom epiphany! I wondered how often this happens and if it were applicable to waiting around in life. Due to that experience, I pay closer attention when I am in public restrooms. Believe it or not, it has happened at least three other times at different venues. One time, there were only three stalls, and all were empty, yet women waited their turn.

I wondered if this would ever happen in the men's bathroom if they had stalls. Are women politer, more patient, or more accepting? Then once at the mall, there was a single bathroom with a full door where you could not see underneath. A guy was waiting to use the restroom, so I waited behind him. Since I am a line expert, I wasted no time with waiting and immediately asked him if someone was inside. He said yes, sharing that he had tried to push the door open, but it wouldn't budge. I then asked if he physically saw a person go inside the restroom. He said no. I asked if he minded if I tried opening the door. He motioned in agreement. I pushed and leaned my body into the door, and it opened with no one inside.

Is that happening to your business? To your career? Was there an open door that you missed? A product you should have created? A company you should have started? But due to fear or perhaps a lack of resources, a more resourceful person walked right in to your door of opportunity.

When I was in college, I used to drink my slushies through Twizzlers. Years later, licorice straws for slushies are available at movie theaters and 7-Eleven. The idea originated in my head, but I lacked the drive to execute my vision. After all, it wasn't even a product that I thought of as a business, just something I enjoyed. Although life is about enjoying precious moments, stop just talking about promising ideas and implement them.

I guarantee there are opportunities behind closed doors that appear locked. After you lean in, push your creative boundaries and forge ahead. Waiting on a yes is counterproductive when your yes is waiting for you to create it.

Daytime Moon

If you ask ten people if they saw the moon in the sky today, they will say no. Now, if you tell people to look for the moon the next morning and ask those same ten people, they will admit to seeing the moon.

One day, driving to school in the hustle and bustle of my life, my toddler son insisted that he saw the moon. I disagreed with him. As we passionately discussed the topic, I stayed focused on weaving between the rush-hour traffic. Finally, he demanded with a cry, "Mommy, I promise I see the moon. Just look."

I gave the sky a pointless glance, and to my surprise, there was the moon. I couldn't believe it. I thought *well, maybe this is rare*. Then after a discussion with my son, he acknowledged seeing it every morning along the drive to school. In researching science, he was right.

The moon is visible on a clear morning nearly every day, yet most people are surprised to see it or learn that this is a normal occurrence. It was normal to my toddler son, who had not a care in the world except enjoying his ride to school. As each of us hustles through life, we undoubtedly miss open doors. Did you happen to capture the moon today?

11

Pay the Yes Forward
| Creative Altruism

WHEN YOUR DREAMS ARE not coming to fruition as you had planned, extend a yes to someone else. As a matter of fact, have a yes day! A colleague, mentee, or even a mentor may need your assistance. Collectively working on other people's goals increases the chances that you will obtain success. This is particularly true when it comes to working for a company.

Your ability to effectively serve your employer

provides you with experience in managing people, projects, conflicts, and stress. In your current position, you have an opportunity to gain specialized information and contacts while utilizing and enhancing your skill set.

Outside work, take the time to assist a family member with a few simple tasks. Offering your time may bring you a sense of joy or satisfaction, which can be used to fuel the momentum that you'll need to accomplish a goal.

Even if a task seems beneath your skill level, such as drafting a handwritten letter or selecting a flower arrangement as a gift, successful leaders value projects completed by their team. No one achieves greatness alone.

Blockbuster movies are a prime example of massive collaboration. You've seen the ending credits. No matter if you were Tom Cruise's driver or the director, you receive credit on the film. One of my first tasks as an assistant after I moved to Los Angeles was to purchase ballet slippers for my boss's daughter. At the time, I had recently earned my bachelor's degree in industrial and operations engineering from the University of Michigan. Although I was genuinely excited to shop for the slippers because I worked for an admired company, you can imagine how my parents felt at the time.

Active Support

Not everyone who needs help will ask for it. Play an active role in a person's support system, whether it's serving as an occasional caretaker, sending motivational texts, proofreading a colleague's work presentation, offering advice about a serious conversation that a friend is going to have with their boss, or serving as a silent sounding board for those with an important speech, sales presentation, or pitch meeting.

Forwarding a newly posted job opening may be life altering to a struggling coworker. Emails that read

"FYI, you may be interested" are often well received, even if the person decides not to apply. Opportunities sometimes arrive in your inbox for you to tap forward.

When prominent executives are tapped for C-level opportunities, such as running a start-up that's heavily backed or overseeing a new division at a competitor, they often hire a team of people who have stood in their corner throughout various stages in their career. Loyalty starts from the initial interaction. It is the enduring commitment through seasons of a person's life trajectory that deems a person trustworthy.

Everyone believes that lending a helping hand and charity work are altruistic. But when you receive a yes, pay it forward within the specific area where you want to thrive, whether that's in the community or workplace.

Creative altruism within your profession will reward you with unpredictable opportunities. Helping others to achieve their dreams will bring you closer to your goals. Invest in a mentee's career, even if it seems pointless. Even simpler, try a new food item on a menu that the waiter suggests so that he hears one less rejection. Advocate for someone else's yes.

The Coffee Test

I once conducted a survey by texting sixty people the same question.

I asked, "If you were a barista and you were required to sell the next customer a cup of coffee, but they didn't drink coffee, what would you do?"

Fifty-eight people said some version of trying to convince the person how amazing coffee is, whether because of its health benefits or the taste of a new flavor. One person said they would beg the customer to purchase a coffee because their job was on the line. Finally, one person said that she would tell the customer to buy it for the next customer. Bingo!

The financial guru who suggested that answer had a yearly sales performance of $1.5 million in volume as an individual effort, and she's also my mother. That explains our #YesDNA. Just as charitable donations come back to you on tax returns, the recipient of a paid-forward yes may be your greatest advocate in helping you achieve uber success.

After the Breakthrough

When you create your own opportunities, you rarely have a ceiling. In fact, the opportunities are endless without restrictions. Be careful not to spend too much time in the planning phase. Entrepreneurs spend enormous amounts of time and energy on how to achieve a breakthrough and a significantly shorter amount of time on what to do after accomplishing a benchmark.

When you achieve breakthrough success, the

hardest thing is to repeat it or surpass it. One-hit wonders are widely referenced in music. The phenomenon happens not only in entertainment but equally in business and technology. Success is not a final destination. NBA teams view success as the momentum needed to three-peat it.

To succeed beyond expectations requires planning for the breakthrough and beyond. When you think of your inchstones and milestones, account for what success will look like in your life when it arrives. What steps will you need to take? Do you have a financial planner or an attorney in case lawsuits arise?

Entrepreneurs are thrilled when an investor says yes, but then they aren't prepared for how to maintain the relationship with their investors or financing entities throughout the business's development process. It's difficult to prepare for something you have never experienced, such as managing people or business partnerships.

You are not expected to predict every life turn or

business fail, but this is what makes advocates incredibly valuable. They can offer suggestions based on their failures and successes. Always listen to them, then decide for yourself the actual solutions for your challenges. Looking through the lens of leaders, you gain insights of what work-life balance looks like in motion, not in theory.

12

Dive In!
| Beyond the Bucket List

THE BEST ETIQUETTE FOR dealing with rejection is to extract its life lessons. Epic fails display the bravery required to passionately pursue dreams while making footprints in the sand, snow, and concrete. If you are exhausted by hearing no, dive deep into life.

Don't overthink what diving in means. Just take action. Make an extreme bucket list for your professional and personal life. For your career, this might include participating in a niche international conference.

If you can't afford to attend, hang out in the lobby of a conference like the American Film Market in Santa Monica, even if you are not an entertainment professional. Talk to every single person with a name tag. Slither out of your zone and get your rejection on!

Take on a second job. Start a company this weekend. Sign up for a media boot camp. Buy a website domain for a business concept that you've talked about but never launched. If your line of work isn't fulfilling, sign up for a university's certificate program to gain skills in a new field. Watch Udemy videos. Write an article on LinkedIn and start authentically connecting to engaging professionals. Design a new app like Udemy meets Snapchat.

Alternate Routines

I don't believe that receiving a yes is a numbers game, but if it is, when your digit is on deck, will you be ready? Get off the hamster wheel. Switch up your routines. Take the streets to work instead of the freeway. If you are working out in the mornings, work out during lunchtime. If you sit on the right side of church, sit on the left. There is proven science behind the positive effects of switching routines to foster creativity. Try a cup of green tea even though you hate it.

If you drive to work the same way, call the same people, drink the same beverages, arrive home to the same roommates, you get the point. More of the same isn't helping you to create yeses. Consistency is an admirable quality, as is loyalty. But you don't want to consistently be loyal to unhappiness and defeat.

Expand beyond what you know and challenge the norm. Wisdom can stifle your ability to generate innovative ideas. There is certainly much to gain by following certain rules or implementing advice from mentors. But be sure to try what seems impossible, just as I did when cold emailing a president at Lionsgate. Dealing with hardships imparts takeaways for your future, not your hindsight.

If you feel anxious in your personal life, switch from yoga to boxing or join a local league team sport. Register for a rock climbing or paddleboard class. Watch an inspiring Netflix documentary, then connect on LinkedIn and Twitter with the experts and documentarian. Identify what inspires you. Then allow the inspiration to permeate your life in the form of action. Create a 360-degree yes map. Take efficient steps toward your milestones.

Think of a way to test your endurance. Maybe it's going to a trampoline park or indoor skydiving. For me, it was diving into the McDonald's dumpster after the restaurant was closed. That's right, totally disgusting, I know, standing in piled-high trash. I think it's the craziest thing I have ever done by choice.

Almost a Millionaire

You may know the Monopoly board game McDonald's has where you collect Monopoly pieces based on your purchases. If you collect certain properties, you get a free menu item. If you collect the dark-blue set of Boardwalk and Park Place, you win a million dollars.

I had the Park Place piece at home, or so I thought, until I received Boardwalk. I was thrilled at first and showed my coworker Matthew, saying, "Oh my gosh, I think I just won a million dollars, because I have the Park Place piece at home."

He responded, "No, that's not possible."

Rethinking the situation, I said, "Yeah, I don't think it's possible either."

I convinced myself that there was no way I had just won a million dollars. I declared that I had mixed things up and was just confused. I dismissively threw away Boardwalk. When I got home, I soon realized that I had just thrown away the winning piece.

So what did I do? I called up Matthew, screaming incoherently at first. Then I asked him if he'd go with me to the dumpster if I split the money with him. He agreed. So Matthew and I went to the McDonald's after it was closed and dived in.

Trust Your Instincts

As I'm sure you can imagine, the dumpster digging was disgusting and draining. We dug for over four hours straight. Suddenly, a police car flashed its lights.

An officer slowly approached us with his flashlight blaring and asked, "What are you doing?"

I explained the situation, and he said, "Keep on digging!"

Sadly, we did not find the piece. I know! What I took away was a million-dollar lesson: trust my instincts. The second thing I learned was even more important. After my sixth shower that night, I discovered my resilience. I had to eventually stop digging and accept the brutal loss. Sometimes a no will be a hard no, and there's no way to change it. That's why the power of creation is priceless. It's never about waiting on a yes. You must find it or make it happen.

What's Near You?

Remember to pay close attention to your surroundings. Take a step back at work to notice the companies in your building or nearby. Look for patterns and things out of the ordinary. Find out who drives the smallest electric car or super car in your company's parking lot. Get to truly know the people in your neighborhood, at your cleaners, barber shop, nail salon, or bank. You are where you are for a reason, so try to find out the connection.

An administrative professional hated her minimum-wage job. One day coming back from lunch, she overheard loud music in the office adjacent to hers. She opened the company's office door and observed the employees celebrating. The consulting firm had just landed a *Fortune* 500 client. She asked if they had any job openings, and they did because of the newly signed business deal. She applied that week and is now their hiring manager.

Are you tired of waiting on a yes? What are you on the verge of quitting? Identify potential advocates and collaborate. Partnerships are a crucial component to elevation in business, career, and personal endeavors. Achieving success is not a science; it is an art form that is mastered through massive rejection.

It's obvious that you are willing to dive in for what you want out of life, or you wouldn't have picked up this book. So the next time that you hear no, don't let it be a permanent setback. And when you keep on hearing no, over and over again, create your own yes!

Acknowledgments

Alexander, Alyssa, and Andrew, I'll never forget coming home one day and you asked me for a treat from the snack drawer.

I said, "No."

You guys continued asking over and over again, adding "please" and then "pretty."

I sternly replied, "I said no. So why are you still asking?"

Alyssa, you announced with a grin, "We are creating our yes!"

Kiddos, you're the best! Keep striving, stay humble, and live happily.

Arthur, thanks for keeping my love tank full.

To my agent, Jim; my editors, Meg and Grace; and the Sourcebooks team—#Yesssss.

Katrina and Bernice, I am grateful for having a chance to give a TEDx Talk. To my BReaKiNG iNTo HoLLyWooD board members, members, and affiliates, let's continue to thrive together!

JC, thank you for this opportunity and for everyone I love.

About the Author

Photo by Randi Laney-Vieira

With more than fifteen years of experience in the entertainment industry, Angela Marie Hutchinson has worked for MGM, Warner Bros. Television, and the Grammys. She is a TEDx speaker and filmmaker. Angela's platform elevated to 90 million viewers when the BBC invited her to be a TV commentator for live coverage of Hollywood's most prestigious night, the 90th Academy Awards on BBC World News.

Angela earned her BSE in industrial and operations engineering from the University of Michigan. Currently, she is a social media professor at Loyola Marymount University in Los Angeles.

As a casting director, Angela has cast veteran actors such as Billy Dee Williams and Lynne Whitfield. The first feature film that Angela produced, wrote, and cast, *Hollywood Chaos*, starred Vanessa Simmons and aired on Hulu. She also directed and produced the PBS documentary *H.U.S.H.*, about Hollywood's uncovered sexual harassment, prior to the #MeToo movement.

For nearly a decade, Angela has continued to produce a diverse portfolio with her media company, BiH Entertainment. She also works as a career coach, public speaker, and business consultant. In 2005, Angela founded BReaKiNG iNTo HoLLyWooD, a 501(c)(3) nonprofit organization that helps entertainment professionals pursue their careers. She has been recognized as a media and arts trailblazer by the U.S. Congress, Los Angeles mayor, and Los Angeles city council. In her leisure time, Angela enjoys Rollerblading and spending time with her rocket scientist husband of fifteen years and their three young children.

NEW! Only from Simple Truths®

IGNITE READS

spark impact in just one hour

IGNITE READS IS A NEW SERIES OF 1-HOUR READS WRITTEN BY WORLD-RENOWNED EXPERTS!

These captivating books will help you become the best version of yourself, allowing for new opportunities in your personal and professional life. Accelerate your career and expand your knowledge with these powerful books written on today's hottest ideas.

TRENDING BUSINESS AND PERSONAL GROWTH TOPICS

 Read in an hour or less

 Leading experts and authors

 Bold design and captivating content